YEAR ONE

UPPER SCHOOL BIBLE WORKBOOK

THE PARABLES OF JESUS

Year One Upper School Bible Workbook: The Parables of Jesus

Nyansa Classical Community Year One Bible Workbook
Copyright © 2026 by Nyansa Classical Community

Scripture quotations are from the American Standard Version

Published in the United States by Nyansa Classical Community
2416 S. Derbigny St.
New Orleans, LA 70125
nyansaclassicalcommunity.org

To order additional materials, please go to www.nyansaclassicalcommunity.com

ISBN 978-1-967443-22-2 (paperback)
ISBN: 978-1-967443-23-9(eBook)

Cover design by Melissa Matos
Book design by Sarah Scudder
Written by Sarah Scudder
Bible Illustrations by Malachi Stonehouse and Jan van t Hoff

Printed in the United States of America

Credit:

Lessons designed by Sarah Scudder

Formatting and Design by Sarah Scudder

Bible Illustrations: Malachi Stonehouse and Jan van t Hoff

Acknowledgements

Thank you to the following organizations for their support and funding:

Upper School Year One Bible

Our Curricula and Programming aim to:

- Cultivate the poetic and moral imaginations
- Deepen delight and enjoyment of classical literature, language, and art
- Tell classic stories using culturally and ethnically diverse images that resonate with young people from a variety of backgrounds
- Encourage students to cultivate truth, goodness, and beauty

NYANSA CLASSICAL COMMINITY

Nyansa Classical Community provides classical, Christian curricula and programming designed to connect with and draw students from diverse backgrounds into the beauty of classical literature and the Great Conversation.

Upper School Year One Bible Workbook

The Parables of Jesus

Jesus' Stories Change How You See the World

Each week's lesson includes the following:

Reading of a parable. Overview and explanation of the parable.

Individual journaling and discussion of the parable.

Memorization of Bible verses.

The study of a historical figure.

This workbook is Designed to be used alongside our Upper School Year One Bible Teacher's Guide. In the Teacher's Guide you will find the complete lessons which include discussion questions, Bible text, and more. To order this curriculum you can go to our website at nyansaclassicalcommunity.org.

This workbook contains journaling pages and discussion questions. The workbook is designed to help the student engage carefully alongside each lesson from our Teacher's Guide.

The symbols identify which section or activity they are currently working through.

For additional resources you can follow the QR code below.

TABLE OF CONTENTS

Week 1:
Parable of the Sowers
Theme: Jesus' Story Changes How You See Your Heart

READ:
Luke 8:4-15

MEMORIZE:
Luke 8:15 And that in the good ground, these are such as in an honest and good heart, having heard the word, hold it fast, and bring forth fruit with patience.

DISCUSSION QUESTIONS:
1. What are the four types of soil? (the hard path, the shallow soil, the thorny soil, good soil)
2. What is the seed the farmer is sowing?
3. What is the gospel? This is a good time to share with the students the Gospel of Christ.
4. What kind of heart do each of the soils represent? (The hard path, the shallow soil, the thorns, and the good soil?)
5. What is the central truth of this parable?

WEEK 1: JOURNALING PROMPTS

In writing, narrate the Parable of the Sower.

# WEEK 1: JOURNALING PROMPTS

In every passage of Scripture we look at the answers to two questions:

What does this passage say about God?

What does this passage say about me?

Week 1: Historical Figure Marva Collins

 **DISCUSSION**

1. What virtues did you see exhibited by Marva Collins?
2. What vices did you see exhibited in her story?
3. How would you compare the Marva Collins story to the parable of "The Soils"?

"Marva Collins served her community well for years, encouraging her students to know that they had value and worth and could succeed."

WEEK 1: JOURNALING PROMPTS

Take time now to reflect. What do you think about the Parable of the Sower? What kind of heart do you have?

The theme of this passage is Jesus' story changes how you see your heart. What kind of heart do you want to have? Why? What are strategies or methods you can use to transform your heart?

WEEK 1: JOURNALING PROMPTS

Write a prayer.

Week 2:
Parable of The Wise and Foolish Builders

Theme: Jesus' Story Changes the Foundation of Your Life

READ:
Matthew 7:24-27

MEMORIZE:
Matthew 7:24 Every one therefore that heareth these words of mine, and doeth them, shall be likened unto a wise man, who built his house upon the rock:

DISCUSSION QUESTIONS:
1. What is the foundation of the wise builder?
2. What is the foundation of the foolish builder?
3. What is Jesus comparing the building to?
4. What is Jesus comparing the rock to?
5. What is Jesus comparing the sand to?
6. What are some of the things of this world that people build their life on?
7. What is the central truth of this story?

In writing, narrate the Parable of the Wise and Foolish Builder.

WEEK 2: JOURNALING PROMPTS

In every passage of Scripture we look at the answers to two questions:

What does this passage say about God?

What does this passage say about me?

Week 2: Historical Figure Sequoyah

DISCUSSION

1. What virtues do you see in Sequoyah?
2. How does his work compare to the wise or foolish builder?
3. What kind of builder do you think Sequoyah was?

"Through Sequoyah's hard work and dedication, the Cherokee people began to use written language to aid in the forming of the Cherokee government. This Cherokee Nation formed a tribal council and even a supreme court."

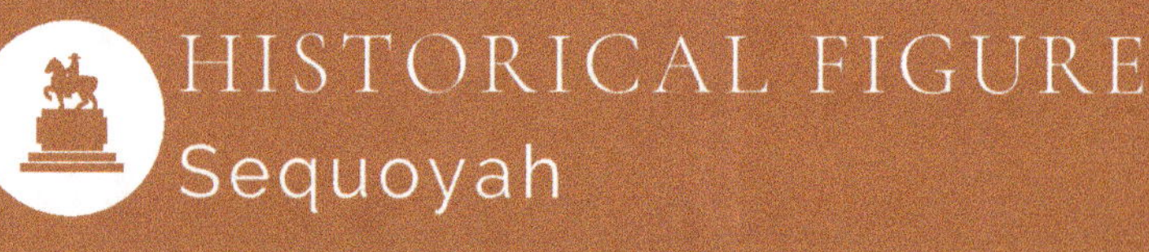

HISTORICAL FIGURE
Sequoyah

WEEK 2: JOURNALING PROMPTS

Take time right now to reflect. What do you think about the "Parable of the Wise and Foolish Builders"?

Why would it be foolish to build your foundation on this world?

WEEK 2: JOURNALING PROMPTS

Why would it be wise to build your life on Jesus?

___

The theme for this week is that Jesus challenges the foundation of your life, which foundation have you built your life on?

___

Is it possible to change your foundation? Why or why not?

___

Write a prayer.

READ:
Luke 7:36-50

MEMORIZE:
Luke 7:47 Wherefore I say unto thee, Her sins, which are many, are forgiven; for she loved much: but to whom little is forgiven, the same loveth little.

DISCUSSION QUESTIONS:
1. Who is Jesus comparing the moneylender to?
2. Who is Jesus comparing the debtor who owed 500 denarii?
3. Who is Jesus comparing the debtor who owed 50 denarii?
4. Is Jesus saying that some sin is worth more? What is Jesus saying? Whose sin needs forgiveness?
5. Who realized they needed forgiveness? Why?

# WEEK 3: JOURNALING PROMPTS

In writing, narrate the Parable of the Moneylender Forgiving Unequal Debt.

WEEK 3: JOURNALING PROMPTS

In every passage of Scripture we look at the answers to two questions:

What does this passage say about God?

What does this passage say about me?

Week 3: Historical Figure John Newton

DISCUSSION

1. What virtues did John Newton exhibit?

2. What vices did John Newton exhibit?

3. Compare Newton to our parable of "The Moneylender Forgiving Unequal Debts", how are these stories similar? How are they different?

4. Is there a difference between human forgiveness and divine forgiveness?

"Newton, [author of Amazing Grace] understood the magnitude of his sin and was in awe of the forgiveness he received."

# WEEK 3: JOURNALING PROMPTS

Take time right now to reflect. What do you think about "The Moneylender Forgiving Unequal Debtors"?

Do you need to be forgiven? Have you sought forgiveness from God?

WEEK 3: JOURNALING PROMPTS

How do you view your sin?

How have you shown forgiveness in your own life? Reflect on a time when you forgave someone that wronged you. How did that make you feel? Was it a difficult process?

# WEEK 3: JOURNALING PROMPTS

Write a prayer.

Week 4:
Parable of The Rich Fool
Building His Bigger Barn
Theme: Jesus' Story Changes How
You Plan Your Future

READ:
Luke 12:13-21

MEMORIZE:
Mark 8:36 For what doth it profit a man, to gain the whole world, and forfeit his life?

DISCUSSION QUESTIONS:
1. Why would Jesus follow his parable with Luke 12:22-34?
2. Look carefully at vs. 24. Who is he reminding us of here in this verse?
3. Where did the rich man put his trust? Where should we put our trust?
4. The rich man was not condemned for his possessions. However, he was condemned for where he placed his trust. He found his safety in his possessions. Jesus is saying that our safety, our surety, our future lies in trusting Him. Discuss.
5. Why can it be scary for some people to put their trust in Jesus versus things on earth?
6. Look at the memory verse for today? How does this apply to today's parable?

WEEK 4: JOURNALING PROMPTS

In writing, narrate the Parable of the Rich Fool Building His Bigger Barn.

WEEK 4: JOURNALING PROMPTS

In every passage of Scripture we look at the answers to two questions:

What does this passage say about God?

____

What does this passage say about me?

____

Week 4: Historical Figure Amanda Berry Smith

 **DISCUSSION**

1. What virtue or virtues does Amanda exhibit?
2. What vices did you see in the reading for today? Who exhibited these vices?
3. How would you compare Amanda's life to the Rich Fool?
4. Could Amanda have shown Calvin and James the errors in their ways? Why or why not?

"Amanda did not pursue the bigger barns of this life, but instead desired the riches she found in serving God, teaching his word, and loving others to Christ."

HISTORICAL FIGURE
Amanda Berry Smith

WEEK 4: JOURNALING PROMPTS

Take time right now to reflect. What do you think about "The Fool Building His Bigger Barns"?

What made the rich man a fool? What is foolishness?

How could the rich man be wise?

WEEK 4: JOURNALING PROMPTS

What are strategies that you can use to show that a "rich man" is being a fool? Do you think people can change their ways?

What are you trusting in? Are you foolish or wise?

# WEEK 4: JOURNALING PROMPTS

Write a prayer.

Week 5:
Parable of The Hidden Treasure; Valuable Pearl

Theme: Jesus' Story Changes What You Value

READ:
Matthew 13:44-46

MEMORIZE:
Philippians 3:8 Yea verily, and I count all things to be loss for the excellency of the knowledge of Christ Jesus my Lord: for whom I suffered the loss of all things, and do count them but refuse, that I may gain Christ

DISCUSSION QUESTIONS:
1. What is the greatest treasure?
2. What would you sacrifice to gain it?
3. What are some things Jesus might be referring to when he says, "sells all he has"?
4. Have you ever sacrificed anything for God? Why is it hard to sacrifice treasure for God? What challenges did you face, and how did you overcome them?
5. What is the central truth of this parable?

# WEEK 5: JOURNALING PROMPTS

In writing, narrate the Parable of the Hidden Treasure and Valuable Pearl.

 # WEEK 5: JOURNALING PROMPTS

In every passage of Scripture we look at the answers to two questions:

What does this passage say about God?

____

____

____

____

What does this passage say about me?

____

____

____

____

Week 5: Historical Figure Jim Elliot

 **DISCUSSION**

1. What virtue(s) did Jim Elliot exhibit?
2. How would you compare Jim Elliot's life to the man who found the treasure or the pearl merchant?
3. Were there any vices in our story for today? Who exhibited them?

"He is no fool who gives what he cannot keep to gain that which he cannot lose." – Jim Elliot

HISTORICAL FIGURE
Jim Elliot

 # WEEK 5: JOURNALING PROMPTS

Take time right now to reflect. What do you think about "The Hidden Treasure" and "The Valuable Pearl"?

What do you find valuable? Does it bring you joy?

Why would Jesus compare the pearl and hidden treasure to the kingdom of heaven?

WEEK 5: JOURNALING PROMPTS

What would you sacrifice to gain the kingdom of heaven?

Compare Philippians 3:8 to the parable. How is Paul similar to the pearl merchant or to the man who found the treasure?

Compare the parable from last week (the Rich Fool) with the parable this week. What are some similarities and differences? How are the parables in conversation with one another?

WEEK 5: JOURNALING PROMPTS

Write a prayer.

Week 6:
Parable of The Lost Sheep; Lost Coin

Theme: Jesus' Story Changes How You See Other

READ:
Luke 15:1-7

MEMORIZE:
Luke 15:7 I say unto you, that even so there shall be joy in heaven over one sinner that repenteth, more than over ninety and nine righteous persons, who need no repentance.

DISCUSSION QUESTIONS:
1. What sacrifices did the shepherd looking for the sheep and the woman looking for the coin make to find their lost possession?
2. The Pharisees refer to the people Jesus is with as sinners, but how does Jesus refer to them? (lost)
3. Why would Jesus call them lost? Who are they lost from?
4. Who is celebrating over the found people?
5. What is the central truth of this parable?

In writing, narrate the Parable of the Lost Sheep and Lost Coin.

WEEK 6: JOURNALING PROMPTS

In every passage of Scripture we look the answer two questions:

What does this passage say about God?

____

____

____

____

What does this passage say about me?

____

____

____

____

Week 6: Historical Figure Gabriela Mistral

 **DISCUSSION**

1. What virtues did you see exhibited in Gabriela Mistral? What vices?
2. How does Gabriela Mistral's life compare to the parable of "The Lost Sheep" or "The Lost Coin" ?
3. What is the power of art, like poetry and literature, to improve the world? Use examples from Gabriela Mistral and from your own knowledge/research.

Gabriela used the struggles of her childhood and feelings of abandonment to write her poetry. She wanted to help other children who might have similar backgrounds and were hurt by rough circumstances.

HISTORICAL FIGURE
Gabriela Mistral

WEEK 6: JOURNALING PROMPTS

Take time right now to reflect. What do you think about "The Lost Sheep" and "The Lost Coin"?

What does it mean to be lost?

How does Jesus show compassion to the lost? How does he show compassion to the Pharisee?

 # WEEK 6: JOURNALING PROMPTS

How does it feel to receive compassion? How does it feel to give compassion?

Who in your life should you show compassion? List 5 practical ways you could show compassion to that person this week?

WEEK 6: JOURNALING PROMPTS

Write a prayer.

Week 7:
Parable of The Prodigal Son
Theme: Jesus' Story Changes How You See God

READ:
Luke 15:11-32

MEMORIZE:
2 Peter 3:9 The Lord is not slack concerning his promise, as some count slackness; but is longsuffering to you-ward, not wishing that any should perish, but that all should come to repentance."

DISCUSSION QUESTIONS:
1. Who is the father in the story representing in the parable?
2. Who is the younger son (the prodigal) representing in the parable?
3. Who is the older son representing in the parable?
4. How does the father show his compassion for his younger son?
5. How does the father show his compassion for his older son?
6. How is Jesus showing compassion to his audience?
7. How does Jesus show his compassion to you?
8. What do you think happened between the brothers after the feast?
9. What is the central truth of this parable?

 WEEK 7: JOURNALING PROMPTS

In writing, narrate the Parable of the Prodigal Son.

WEEK 7: JOURNALING PROMPTS

In every passage of Scripture we look the answer two questions:

What does this passage say about God?

What does this passage say about me?

Week 7: Historical Figure Herb Lusk

DISCUSSION

1. What virtues did you see exhibited in Herb Lusk?
2. How does Herb Lusk's life compare to the parable of "The Prodigal Son"? Are there similarities? Are there differences?
3. How do you think Herb Lusk's teammates' and coaches' feelings changed after they saw him work in the ministry? What about his fans?

Many people told Lusk that he was taking a step down when he left football to become a pastor, but Lusk never regretted his decision.

HISTORICAL FIGURE
Herb Lusk

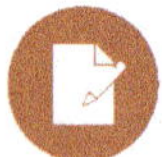

WEEK 7: JOURNALING PROMPTS

Take time right now to reflect. What do you think about "The Prodigal Son"?

How do you see God showing compassion to you?

What are some ways that you show compassion to others?

WEEK 7: JOURNALING PROMPTS

Who are some people you struggle to show compassion to?

Are you the prodigal son or the older brother? In what ways?

As we stated on Day 1, this is one of the most famous, if not the most famous, parable. Why do you think that is? What is so powerful about this story?

WEEK 7: JOURNALING PROMPTS

Write a prayer.

Week 8:

Parable of The Unmerciful Servant

Theme: Jesus' Story Changes How You Forgive

READ:
Matthew 18:21-34

MEMORIZE:
Ephesians 4:32 and be ye kind one to another, tenderhearted, forgiving each other, even as God also in Christ forgave you.

DISCUSSION QUESTIONS:
1. What does the debt represent?
2. Who does the king represent? Who do the debtors represent?
3. What does this parable reveal about the nature of man?
4. What does this parable reveal about the nature of divine forgiveness?
5. What does this parable reveal about the nature of our forgiveness when compared to the forgiveness of God?
6. Think about the statement that opened up the overview, "forgive and forget". What are your thoughts on this manner of forgiveness? Are there some grievances that should be forgotten? How do you distinguish between them?
7. Read the memory verse for today. Compare what Paul says in Ephesians 4:32 to the parable. How are they saying the same thing?
8. What is the central truth of this parable?

# WEEK 8: JOURNALING PROMPTS

In writing, narrate the Parable of the Unmerciful Servant.

WEEK 8: JOURNALING PROMPTS

In every passage of Scripture we look at the answers to two questions:

What does this passage say about God?

What does this passage say about me?

Week 8: Historical Figure Vincent Guerrero

DISCUSSION

1. What virtues or vices did you see exhibited in Vincent Guerrero?
2. How does Vincent Guerrero's life compare to the parable of "The Unmerciful Servant"? Are there similarities? Are there differences?
3. Is there a place for mercy and forgiveness and war? How could they work together? How are they opposites of each other?
4. Are there other historical figures that remind you of Vincent Guerrero? How are they similar? How are they different?

Guerrero, [the second president of Mexico], abolished slavery. He also supported the start of public schools, reform for land ownership, and more.

HISTORICAL FIGURE
Vincent Guerrero

WEEK 8: JOURNALING PROMPTS

Take time right now to reflect. What do you think about "The Unmerciful Servant"?

How do you see God's forgiveness toward you?

Have you ever been forgiven? How did being forgiven make you feel? What actions did you have to take to gain that forgiveness? How did asking for forgiveness make you feel?

# WEEK 8: JOURNALING PROMPTS

Is there someone you feel like you can't forgive? What makes their actions so heinous?

How has this parable changed your views on forgiveness?

Write a letter to someone you need to forgive.

WEEK 8: JOURNALING PROMPTS

Write a prayer.

Week 9:
Parable of The Good Samaritan
Theme: Jesus' Story Changes How You Help

READ:
Luke 10:25-37

MEMORIZE:
Luke 10:27 Thou shalt love the Lord thy God with all thy heart, and with all thy soul, and with all thy strength, and with all thy mind; and thy neighbor as thyself.

DISCUSSION QUESTIONS:
1. How was the lawyer trying to "justify himself" with his question?
2. How do you think the man felt when the priest and the Levite passed him by?
3. What are some reasons that the priest and the Levite might give for not helping the fallen man?
4. Who in the story was the most compassionate?
5. Why would Jesus choose a Samaritan to be the hero of the story?
6. What does Jesus mean by "go and do likewise"?
7. What is the central truth of this parable?

# WEEK 9: JOURNALING PROMPTS

In writing, narrate the Parable of the Good Samaritan.

WEEK 9: JOURNALING PROMPTS

In every passage of Scripture we look the answer two questions:

What does this passage say about God?

____

____

____

____

What does this passage say about me?

____

____

____

____

Week 9: Historical Figure Juana Ines de la Cruz

 **DISCUSSION**

1. What virtues or vices did you see exhibited in Juana Ines de la Cruz?
2. How does Juana Ines' life compare to the parable of "The Good Samaritan"? Are there similarities? Are there differences? Were there other people in her life that show a similarity to the characters in the parable.

[Juana Ines] saw her intellect as a gift to be used for God and developed her skills throughout her life. Juana Ines taught many women about the gospel and reached out to many of the poor people of Mexico.

WEEK 9: JOURNALING PROMPTS

Take time right now to reflect. What do you think about "The Good Samaritan"?

Who is your neighbor? Who are the people in your life God has called you to love?

What are ways that you could help others around you? Make a list of ways you could help: your family, your church, your community, your school.

WEEK 9: JOURNALING PROMPTS

The former British Prime Minister Margaret Thatcher once said of this parable, "No one would remember the Good Samaritan if he'd only had good intentions-he had money as well." What are your thoughts on this statement? Does it take means (like money and earthly goods) to be a Good Samaritan? What are some ways you can be a Good Samaritan, even if you don't have much to give?

WEEK 9: JOURNALING PROMPTS

Write a prayer.

Week 10:
Parable of The Rich Man and Lazarus

Theme: Jesus' Story Changes How You See Death

READ:
Luke 16:19-31

MEMORIZE:
Micah 6:8 He hath showed thee, O man, what is good; and what doth Jehovah require of thee, but to do justly, and to love kindness, and to walk humbly with thy God?

DISCUSSION QUESTIONS:
1. Using the five principles above, discuss what does this parable reveal about what happens to us when we die?
2. Why is the rich man in our story condemned? What does the parable reveal about his sin?
3. How should we view our death? How should we live in light of death?
4. What is the central truth of this parable?

WEEK 10: JOURNALING PROMPTS

In writing, narrate the Parable of the Rich Man and Lazarus.

 # WEEK 10: JOURNALING PROMPTS

In every passage of Scripture we look at the answers to two questions:

What does this passage say about God?

What does this passage say about me?

Week 10: Historical Figure William Booth

DISCUSSION

1. What virtues or vices did you see exhibited in William Booth?

2. How does William Booth's life compare to the parable of "The Rich Man and Lazarus"? Are there similarities? Are there differences? Were there other people in her life that show a similarity to the characters in the parable?

3. How do you think William Booth's experience as a pawnbroker contributed to his worldview? Think about the types of people who pawn items and how they feel when their items are sold.

Through his ministry to the poor, William Booth opened the East London Christian Mission [now known as the Salvation Army] in 1865.

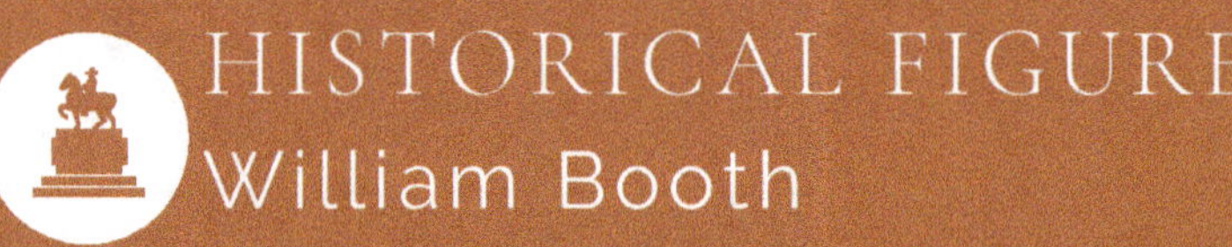

# WEEK 10: JOURNALING PROMPTS

Take time right now to reflect. What do you think about "The Good Samaritan"?

How has this parable changed your thoughts about death?

Have you ever been like the Rich Man, walking past a figure like Lazarus? Reflect on a time in your life where you may have been called on to do more to help others.

WEEK 10: JOURNALING PROMPTS

What is your life about? Do you spend time and energy on helping others who are in need? Or are you making your life about clothes, food, friends, etc?

What are your thoughts on Abraham's statement at the end of the parable, "If they hear not Moses and the prophets, neither will they be persuaded, if one rise from the dead."? Are there some people who can't be convinced to do the right thing? Are they lost causes?

WEEK 10: JOURNALING PROMPTS

Write a prayer and ask God to reveal what you are living for.

Week 11:
Parable of The Lowest Seat at the Feast
Theme: Jesus' Story Changes Your Ambition

READ:
Luke 14:7-11

MEMORIZE:
Luke 14:11 For every one that exalteth himself shall be humbled; and he that humbleth himself shall be exalted.

DISCUSSION QUESTIONS:
1. Compare and contrast Luke 14:7-11 with Luke 22: 24-30. What do you notice?
2. How is God's kingdom upside down? How does this world view ambition compared to how Jesus views it?
3. What does Jesus' story say about your place in the world?
4. What is humility? What could or should it look like?
5. What is the opposite of humility?
6. Can pride ever be a good thing? Is there a difference between pride and arrogance?
7. Read Philippians 2:3-4. "3 doing nothing through faction or through vainglory, but in lowliness of mind each counting other better than himself; 4 not looking each of you to his own things, but each of you also to the things of others." How does this verse confirm what Jesus taught in his parable?
8. What is the central truth of this parable?

In writing, narrate the Parable of the Lowest Seat at the Feast.

In every passage of Scripture we look at the answer to two questions:

What does this passage say about God?

What does this passage say about me?

Week 11: Historical Sandy F. Rey

DISCUSSION

1. What virtues or vices did you see exhibited in Sandy F. Ray?
2. How does Sandy F. Ray's life compare to the parable of "The Lowest Seat at the Feast"? Are there similarities? Are there differences?
3. What is ambition? How could it hinder what Sandy F. Ray accomplished in his life?
4. How is working in politics, like Sandy Ray did, an example of "a life of service"? Do people always enter politics with noble intentions? Is there a way to differentiate between a politician who has virtue from one who is prideful?

Sandy provided advice and counsel for Martin Luther King Jr., and Ray himself was heavily involved in the Civil Rights Movement.

HISTORICAL FIGURE
Sandy F. Rey

 # WEEK 11: JOURNALING PROMPTS

Take time right now to reflect. What do you think about "The Lowest Seat at the Feast"?

What is your ambition? What do you want to accomplish in life?

Does your ambition align with what Jesus says your ambition in life ought to be?

WEEK 11: JOURNALING PROMPTS

What is humility? What areas do you struggle to be humble?

Thankfully, our streets are much cleaner nowadays (or at least we have better shoes), and washing feet is no longer a task we have to do upon entering a house—though you should still when you shower! What are some ways to "wash someone's feet" in the modern world?

James 4:10 says, "Humble yourselves in the sight of the Lord, and he shall exalt you." How does this verse fit with Jesus' parable?

Write a prayer and ask God to help you with humility.

Week 12:
Parable of The Weeds Among Good Plants
Theme: Jesus' Story Changes Our Judgment

READ:
Matthew 13:24-30, 34-43

MEMORIZE:
I Samuel 16:7b Jehovah seeth not as man seeth; for man looketh on the outward appearance, but Jehovah looketh on the heart.

DISCUSSION QUESTIONS:
1. When Jesus says the "kingdom of heaven" what is he referring to?
2. Compare the story to Jesus' interpretation. Write down the different references of the story to the meaning. For example: The sower is the Son of Man (Jesus).
3. Who in Jesus day looked like followers of Jesus, but were really "sons of the evil one"?
4. Who in our world today might look like followers of Christ, but are just "weeds"?
5. Whose job is it to judge the wheat and the tares? Why is it not our job?
6. Look at today's memory verse, I Samuel 16:7. What does God say about the judging of men?
7. If Jesus' story changes how we judge, who should we judge? What benefit is there in examining our own hearts? Why is it so much harder to judge ourselves than to judge other people?
8. Is being "wheat" or "tare" a static thing, or can people change their nature? Once you are "wheat", are you set for life, or is it a constant process? Why or why not?
9. What is the central truth of this parable?

WEEK 12: JOURNALING PROMPTS

In writing, narrate the Parable of the Weeds Among Good Plants.

WEEK 12: JOURNALING PROMPTS

In every passage of Scripture we look at the answer to two questions:

What does this passage say about God?

What does this passage say about me?

Week 12: Historical Figure Plato

DISCUSSION

1. What virtues or vices did you see exhibited in Plato?

2. How does Plato's life compare to the parable of "The Weeds Among Good Plants"? Are there similarities? Are there differences?

3. What benefits do we experience from Plato's accomplishments?

4. As stated above, much of Plato's writing takes the form of fictional dialogues between Socrates and another character. How is learning in this way easier than learning via standard books/essay? How is it harder?

Plato gave rise to questions for people to ask when thinking about life. His influence is still seen and felt today in education, religion, and philosophy.

HISTORICAL FIGURE
Plato

# WEEK 12: JOURNALING PROMPTS

Take time right now to reflect. What do you think about "The Weeds Among Good Plants"?

Take a moment to judge your own heart? Are you a wheat or a tare? What reasons do you have to make you decide which one you are?

How do you work on not judging others? What are some ways that you remind yourself that it is not for you to judge?

WEEK 12: JOURNALING PROMPTS

Take stock of your life? Why are you following Jesus?

We have now finished our 12 weeks of parables. Which one or two have been the most memorable for you? What about the story made it stick in your head?

WEEK 12: JOURNALING PROMPTS

Write a prayer and ask God to help you see yourself accurately.

Week 13:
Parable of The Early and Late Workers in the Vineyard

Theme: Jesus' Story Changes Your Understanding of Grace

READ:
Matthew 19:27 - 20:16

MEMORIZE:
Matthew 19:30 But many shall be last that are first; and first that are last.

DISCUSSION QUESTIONS:

1. Look at the context of the parable. Who is Jesus talking to in the parable?
2. Why does Peter talk about what he has given up for Jesus? How does that connect with why Jesus tells this parable?
3. What does the parable say about itself? Look at the details of the parable. Who are the characters, what are they doing? What is the sequence of events in the parable: what happened first, next, last?
4. Was it fair for the master to pay the same amount to every worker? Why or why not?
5. Did the master do what he said he would? Does he have the right to give any amount of money to the workers he decides?
6. Was the master unjust in his giving payment? Did any of the workers deserve anything more than what was offered to them?
7. What is the central truth of this parable?

In writing, narrate the Parable of the Early and Late Workers in the Vineyard.

WEEK 13: JOURNALING PROMPTS

In every passage of Scripture we look the answer two questions:

What does this passage say about God?

____

....

....

....

____

What does this passage say about me?

____

....

....

....

____

Week 13: Historical Figure Jerry Pinkney

DISCUSSION

1. What virtues or vices did you see exhibited in Jerry Pinkney?
2. How does Pinkney's life compare to the parable of "The Early and Late Workers in the Vineyard"? Are there similarities? Are there differences?
3. How did Pinkney experience grace in his life? Who were the people who gave Pinkney grace?

In spite of Pinkney's academic struggles, he used his talents and worked hard. His illustrations have been seen by thousands and have been used to bring reading to life for children everywhere.

HISTORICAL FIGURE
Jerry Pinkney

https://en.wikipedia.org/wiki/Jerry_Pinkney

WEEK 13: JOURNALING PROMPTS

Take time right now to reflect. What do you think about "The Early and Late Workers in the Vineyard"?

What is grace? How does the story reflect God's grace?

Reflect. What ways have you seen God's grace in your own life?

How have you shown grace to others? Does it reflect the same grace as seen in this parable?

Write a prayer and ask God to help you understand His grace and then to show grace to others.

Week 14:
Parable of The Widow and the Crooked Judge
Theme: Jesus' Story Changes Your Attitude of Prayer

READ:
Luke 18:1-8

MEMORIZE:
Luke 11:13 If ye then, being evil, know how to give good gifts unto your children, how much more shall your heavenly Father give the Holy Spirit to them that ask him?

DISCUSSION QUESTIONS:
1. Who is this parable addressed to?
2. In the first verse, Jesus says to not lose heart, what does that mean?
3. What does the widow do in the story? How does she come to the judge? What does she ask him for? How does this compare to prayer?
4. Why do you think the judge would wait for a long time before helping the widow? Why did he finally break down? How do you think the widow felt after asking the judge so many times?
5. Why does Jesus compare God to the judge? How are they the same? How are they different?
6. Is there such a thing as blind justice? Can there be?
7. There is a common expression "better late than never". What are your thoughts on the expression? Do you agree or disagree? Why? How do you see it illustrated in the parable?
8. What is the central truth of this parable?
9. For additional discussion, look up Luke 11:5-13 and compare this parable to our parable for today.

WEEK 14: JOURNALING PROMPTS

In writing, narrate the Parable of the Widow and the Crooked Judge.

In every passage of Scripture we look at the answer to two questions:

What does this passage say about God?

____

____

____

____

What does this passage say about me?

____

____

____

____

Week 14: Historical Figure Elizabeth Freeman

DISCUSSION

1. What virtues or vices did you see exhibited in Elizabeth Freeman?
2. How does Freeman's life compare to the parable of "The Persistent Widow and the Crooked Judge"? Are there similarities? Are there differences?
3. What is the importance of precedence, in the legal system and in your own life? Think about the idea of consistency.
4. Stone and monuments can last forever, or at least for a very long time. People, however, can get sick, die before their time, and even if they live a full life only have around 100 years, and oftentimes much less. So what do you think of Pericles' quotes at the beginning of the page? How is a living legacy a stronger one than a material legacy? Is it?
5. What do you think of your legacy? Who are the people around you who have gone before you and helped to shape who you are? Who do you want to influence for the future?

WEEK 14: JOURNALING PROMPTS

Take time right now to reflect. What do you think about "The Persistent Widow and the Crooked Judge"?

How did this parable change the way you thought about prayer?

Have you changed how you have prayed this week? If so, how?

What do you need? Make a list. Remember that, in the parable, the widow was specific in her request versus asking for help generally. Spend some time praying for your needs.

How has this parable changed how you view God? Do you think God wants to hear your prayers?

Week 15:
The Invitation to a Great Banquet and Wedding
Theme: Jesus' Story Changes You Pursue in Life

READ:
Luke 14:15-24

MEMORIZE:
Matthew 22:9-10 Go ye therefore unto the partings of the highways, and as many as ye shall find, bid to the marriage feast. And those servants went out into the highways, and gathered together all as many as they found, both bad and good: and the wedding was filled with guests.

DISCUSSION QUESTIONS:

1. Who is the parable recorded in Luke addressed to? Who is the parable recorded in Matthew addressed to?

2. Compare the two parables. How are they similar? How are they different? Do you believe this is the same parable recorded twice or two different parables? Why?

3. Jesus compares the Kingdom of Heaven to a banquet or a great party. Imagine a wedding reception where there is happiness, feasting, and celebrating. Why would Jesus compare Heaven to this kind of celebration? What are the similarities? What could you imagine would be different from our world's celebrations and what Jesus is referring to as a banquet?

4. Look at how each parable begins. Who is Jesus talking to? How does this give us insight into the meaning of the parables?

5. What excuses did the people give for not coming to the banquet? What does this show about what they wanted to pursue?

6. What pursuits in life keep people from following Jesus? How do the people in the parable compare to the same excuses people give today?

7. In the second parable, how did the people treat the servants from the king? What does this say about how people treat Christ's invitation to follow Jesus?

8. What is the significance of the wedding garment? Why would the man be punished for not wearing the robe provided by the king?

9. What is the central truth of this parable?

WEEK 15: JOURNALING PROMPTS

In writing, narrate the Parable of the The Invitation to a Great Banquet and Wedding.

WEEK 15: JOURNALING PROMPTS

In every passage of Scripture we look the answer two questions:

What does this passage say about God?

____

____

____

____

What does this passage say about me?

____

____

____

____

Week 15: Historical Figure Kathrine Johnson

 **DISCUSSION**

1. What virtues did you see exhibited in Kathrine Johnson?

2. How does Johnson's life compare to the parable of "The Invitation to the Great Banquet" and "The Invitation to the Wedding Banquet"? Are there similarities? Are there differences?

3. What do you think of her invitations to contribute toward society? Do you believe she made the most out of her opportunities?

4. Astronaut John Glenn did not trust the computers' calculations, and required a human to double check the numbers before he felt safe flying. Do you think that would happen today? In an increasingly tech-driven world, what are situations in which we need a human touch? Are there certain things we can't mechanise?

Kathrine Johnson was an incredible woman with an incredible mind.

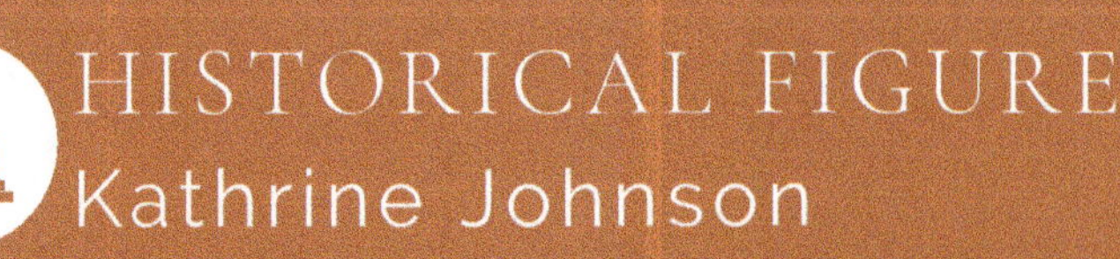

WEEK 15: JOURNALING PROMPTS

Take time right now to reflect. What do you think about "The Invitation to the Great Banquet" and "The Invitation to the Wedding Banquet"?

What are your pursuits? Do they interfere with your pursuit of Jesus? Why or why not?

What excuses have you heard from others or excuses you made yourself as to why you can't pursue Jesus right now in your life?

WEEK 15: JOURNALING PROMPTS

Do you believe that Jesus has given an invitation to you? Do you believe
He has provided you with His righteousness?

Think about the banquet in the parable, and think about Katherine Johnson.
She had to bow out of her degree program, for familial duties. How do you
think the host would feel if someone had to leave the banquet early? How do
you find balance between temporal pursuits and eternal?

Week 16:
Parable of The Talents
Theme: Jesus' Story Changes Our View of Work

READ:
Matthew 25:14-30

MEMORIZE:
Matthew 25:21 His lord said unto him, Well done, good and faithful servant: thou hast been faithful over a few things, I will set thee over many things; enter thou into the joy of thy lord.

DISCUSSION QUESTIONS:
1. Who is this parable addressed to? Remember the audience that Jesus is speaking to helps determine the meaning of the parable. Is he talking to His disciples, the Pharisees, a crowd?
2. Did the master ever directly give instructions to the servants, or were they supposed to "read between the lines"?
3. What was the difference between the three servants?
4. Why did the first two servants profit? Why was the third servant unprofitable?
5. What were the servant's responses to the talents they were given?
6. What did each servant think about their master? And how did that affect what they did with their talents?
7. What was the master's response to the first two servants? What was the master's response to the last servant?
8. What does this parable tell you about how you should work? What tasks are you responsible for? How should you handle them?
9. What is the central truth of this parable?

WEEK 16: JOURNALING PROMPTS

In writing, narrate the Parable of the The Talents.

# WEEK 16: JOURNALING PROMPTS

In every passage of Scripture we look at the answer to two questions:

What does this passage say about God?

What does this passage say about me?

Week 16: Historical Figure Maria Tallchief

 **DISCUSSION**

1. What virtues did you see exhibited in Maria Tallchief?

2. How does Maria Tallchief's life compare to the parable of "The Talents"? Are there similarities? Are there differences?

3. In theater, it's often said "there are no small parts, only small actors". What are your thoughts on this saying? Do you think it applies outside the world of performing arts?

4. What do you think of her invitations to contribute toward society? Do you believe she was faithful in using her abilities?

Throughout her career, Maria was advised to change her Native American name. Others told her she would receive better opportunities if her name sounded Russian. However, Maria Tallchief would not move. She understood and appreciated her heritage.

HISTORICAL FIGURE
Maria Tallchief

WEEK 16: JOURNALING PROMPTS

Take time right now to reflect. What do you think about "The Parable of the Talents"?

What are some abilities you have? How are you using them?

If you do not develop your abilities you often lose the ability altogether. A person who has a great capacity to memorize, finds it harder to remember things if they don't practice the art of memorization. How do you feel about developing your abilities?

____

____

____

____

Do you believe God has a purpose behind the abilities He has given you? How do you think God wants you to use your abilities or talents to serve Him?

____

____

____

____

Week 17:
Parable of The Ten Virgins
Theme: Jesus' Story Changes How You Look for Jesus

READ:
Matthew 25:1-13

MEMORIZE:
Matthew 25:13 Watch therefore, for ye know not the day nor the hour.

DISCUSSION QUESTIONS:
1. Who are the ten virgins representing in our parable?
2. Who does the bridegroom represent?
3. Why do the virgins not know when the groom is coming?
4. How does this relate to us today? Who are we waiting for? Do we know when He is coming?
5. Do we know when Jesus is coming?
6. What does our not knowing when He is coming force us to do?
7. Why were half of the virgins considered wise? What did they do that showed they were being wise?
8. Why were half of the virgins considered foolish? What did they do that showed they were acting foolishly?
9. What do the lamps represent?
10. Look at Matthew chapter 25. Consider the context of the story. Who is Jesus telling this story to? Does this make a difference in who is waiting for the bridegroom?
11. What is the central truth of this parable?

WEEK 17: JOURNALING PROMPTS

In writing, narrate the Parable of the The Ten Virgins.

WEEK 17: JOURNALING PROMPTS

In every passage of Scripture we look at the answer to two questions:

What does this passage say about God?

What does this passage say about me?

 **DISCUSSION**

1. What virtues did you see exhibited in Thomas Andrew Dorsey?

2. How does Thomas Andrew Dorsey's life compare to the parable of "The Ten Virgins"? Are there similarities? Are there differences?

3. Are there ways that Dorsey life shows us how to look for Jesus? What ways did he see Jesus in his life?

4. Dorsey returned to the Church after his fight with a severe illness. Why might that have happened? Is it similar to any other stories you've heard, in your own life or reading, about other returns to Faith?

5. What do you think of the hymn, "Precious Lord, Take My Hand?" Does it have any meaning for you in our life?

> Dorsey took the tragedy in his life and used it to write one of the most beloved hymns we have.

 HISTORICAL FIGURE
Thomas Andrew Dorsey

WEEK 17: JOURNALING PROMPTS

Take time right now to reflect. What do you think about "The Parable of the Ten Virgins"?

Who do you identify with, the wise or foolish virgins? Why?

WEEK 17: JOURNALING PROMPTS

What are you doing to be prepared for Jesus' return?

Do you think being prepared is important? What other ways do you try to build up the virtue of the discipline of preparedness in your school? Home? Church? Try to write a specific plan you could write, to help keep disciplined and to be prepared. This can be for anything, from athletics tryouts to how you can prepare for Jesus' arrival.

Write a prayer.

Week 18:
Parable of The Wise and Foolish Servants
Theme: Jesus' Story Changes How We Act When Alone

READ:
Matthew 24:45-51; Luke 12:42-48

MEMORIZE:
Luke 12:48b And to whomsoever much is given, of him shall much be required: and to whom they commit much, of him will they ask the more.

DISCUSSION QUESTIONS:
1. Who is Jesus telling this story to? Read the context around the passage.
2. Who is the master in this story? What is he like?
3. What are the servants like? How do they act when they feel like no one is watching them?
4. How does the phrase, "When the cat's away, the mice will play." relate to our story today? Have you ever encountered a situation like this, say if a teacher left the room or your parents left an older sibling in charge? How did you react?
5. Do you think the servant in charge would have acted this way with the Master present? Why or why not?
6. What is the conclusion of the story? What does this reveal about the nature of man and the nature of Jesus?
7. What is the central truth of this parable?

In writing, narrate the Parable of the The Wise and Foolish Servants.

 # WEEK 18: JOURNALING PROMPTS

In every passage of Scripture we look the answer two questions:

What does this passage say about God?

____

____

____

____

What does this passage say about me?

____

____

____

____

Week 18: Historical Figure Sophia Brahe

 **DISCUSSION**

1. What virtues did you see exhibited in Sophia Brahe's life?
2. What connections do you see between The Wise and Foolish Servants and Sophia Brahe? Was her character consistent?
3. Some people present science and faith as two different subjects that are opposed. What do you think of this idea? Do you agree or disagree? Is there a place for faith in science? For science in faith?
4. Sophia flourished in part because of the support her older brother, Tycho Brahe, gave her. Who are some people in your own life that have supported you, despite resistance? Have you ever supported someone in their passions?

At the age of seventeen, Sophia began to work with her brother in making scientific observations in astronomy.

HISTORICAL FIGURE
Sophia Brahe

# WEEK 18: JOURNALING PROMPTS

Take time right now to reflect. What do you think about "The Parable of the Wise and Foolish Servants"?

Who do you identify with, the wise or foolish servant? Why?

What is character? What are some virtues that you feel you need to work on?

WEEK 18: JOURNALING PROMPTS

What are you like when no one is watching? How do you treat those you feel are under you? What does this say about your character?

If someone is abusing a position of power, what is your duty? Should you step up and confront them?

Write a prayer.

Week 19:

Parable of The Pharisee and the Tax Collector

Theme: Jesus' Story Changes Our View of Self

READ:
Luke 18:10-14

MEMORIZE:
Luke 18:14 I tell you, this man went down to his house justified, rather than the other. For everyone who exalts himself will be humbled, but the one who humbles himself will be exalted.

DISCUSSION QUESTIONS:

1. Who is Jesus telling this story to? Read the context around the passage.
2. What is the Pharisee like? What is he saying? How does he view himself?
3. What is the Tax Collector like? What is he saying? How does he view himself?
4. Do you think that the Pharisee or the Tax Collector views themself accurately?
5. Is it ever ok to work with an enemy? Tax collectors were hated because they worked for Rome, the colonisers of the Jewish people. Why might they do that?
6. How can we see ourselves accurately? How do we know who we are?
7. We know, from many parables, that you can be too prideful, but can you be too humble? What is the right balance between pride and humility?
8. What is the central truth of this parable?

WEEK 19: JOURNALING PROMPTS

In writing, narrate the Parable of the The Pharisee and Tax Collector.

# WEEK 19: JOURNALING PROMPTS

In every passage of Scripture we look at the answer to two questions:

What does this passage say about God?

____

____

____

____

What does this passage say about me?

____

____

____

____

Week 19: Historical Figure Olaudah Equiano

DISCUSSION

1. What virtues and vices do you see displayed in Equiano's life?
2. What connections do you see between The Pharisee and the Tax Collector and Olaudah Equiano? Was his character consistent?
3. How did Equiano's view of self help him to become a leader to others?
4. Shakespeare has a famous quote in Romeo and Juliet that "a rose by any other name would smell as sweet". What does this quote mean to you? Do you agree or disagree? Why are names so important to us? Why might Equiano have resisted the changing of his name so fiercely?
5. Equiano was not afraid to speak out about his faith and to challenge others in their faith. What do you think gave him the confidence he needed?
6. What are some ways today that people are hypocrites (i.e. like the Christians of Equine's day, who said they were followers of Christ and yet engaged in slavery)? How can you help yourself and others become more consistent in their beliefs and actions?

# WEEK 19: JOURNALING PROMPTS

Take time right now to reflect. What do you think about "The Parable of the Pharisee and Tax Collector"?

Who do you identify with, the Pharisee or the Tax Collector? Why?

How do you view yourself? How would you define yourself?

WEEK 19: JOURNALING PROMPTS

Who does God say that you are? Look up the following verses: Isaiah 53:6; Romans 3:10. What do those verses mean to you?

Write a prayer.

Week 20:
Parable of The Master and His Servant
Theme: Jesus' Story Changes Our Sense of Duty

READ:
Luke 17:5-10

MEMORIZE:
Luke 17:10 Even so ye also, when ye shall have done all the things that are commanded you, say, We are unprofitable servants; we have done that which it was our duty to do.

DISCUSSION QUESTIONS:
1. Who is Jesus telling this story to? Read the context around the passage.
2. Why did Jesus start off the parable talking about faith? What does he say about faith?
3. What is the relationship between faith and duty? Why does a person need faith to obey and serve?
4. Why should the servant not expect to eat with or fellowship with the master?
5. What is the role of a servant? What is their duty? How does that change their relationship to the master?
6. What is the difference between performing a duty versus giving a gift or doing someone a favor?
7. What is the central truth of this parable?

WEEK 20: JOURNALING PROMPTS

In writing, narrate the Parable of the The Master and His Servant.

 # WEEK 20: JOURNALING PROMPTS

In every passage of Scripture we look at the answer to two questions:

What does this passage say about God?

What does this passage say about me?

Week 20: Historical Figure Sophie Scholl

 **DISCUSSION**

1. What virtues and vices do you see in the life of Sophie Scholl?

2. What connections can you make between The Parable of the Master and His Servant and Sophie Scholl?

3. What do you think Sophie was trying to say with her last words?

4. The Nazi's took control of Germany's education system, turning lessons into propaganda. They also made it near mandatory for children to join the Hitler Youth (for boys) or the League of German Girls (for girls). Why do you think the regime was obsessed with controlling the youth? What power do young people have?

5. Why do you think the group called themselves The White Rose? What are some connotations of the color white or of a rose? What about the two combined?

6. What do the words "passive resistance" mean to you? What are some examples you can think of? Is passive resistance effective? Why or why not?

7. What is your duty when you see injustice? How do you stand up for what is right?

HISTORICAL FIGURE
Sophie Scholl

WEEK 20: JOURNALING PROMPTS

Take time right now to reflect. What do you think about "The Parable of the Master and His Servant"?

Why did the disciples ask Jesus to increase their faith? Do you have the same desire? Would you ask Jesus to increase your faith?

What is the relationship between faith and obedience?

WEEK 20: JOURNALING PROMPTS

What are the duties you have in your life? What do you believe you need in order to grow in how you fulfill your duties?

Write a prayer asking God to help you know what and how to complete your duties in life.

IMAGES CREDIT

Week 1:
"Parable of the Sower" Jan van t Hoff, copyright of www.gospelimages.com; used with permission from artist.

"Leaning Tower of Pisa", Photochrom Print Collection, Pisa; Italy, between 1890 and 1900, Public Domain

Week 3:
Vase dedicated to King Unas-E 32372, Unknown artist, between 2380 and 2350 BC, Department of Egyptian Antiquities of the Louvre, Public Domain

Week 6: "The Parable of the Lost Sheep", Jan van t Hoff, copyright of www.gospelimages.com; used with permission from artist.

Week 7: "The Prodigal Son", Jan van t Hoff, copyright of www.gospelimages.com; used with permission from artist.

HISTORICAL FIGURE ARTWORK/PHOTO CREDIT

Week 1: President George W. Bush and Mrs. Laura Bush with National Medal of Humanities Recipient Marva Collins in the Oval Office, 17 November 2004, Collection: Records of the White House Photo Office, Public Domain

Week 2:Henry Inman's Lithograph of Charles Byrd King's original portrait of Sequoyah in The Indian Tribes of North America by McKenney and Hall. From the Georgia Historical Society Rare Collection. Public Domain

Week 3 Joseph Collyer/ After John Russell, John Newton- The Cowper and Newton Museum, Public Domain,

Week 4: Amanda Berry Smith, circa 1885, Albumen silver print. Public Domain.

Week 6: Gabriela Mistral, unknown date, Public Domain

Week 8:A half-length, Posthumous Portrait by Anacleto Escutia (1850), Public Domain

Week 9: Portrait of Sor Juana Inés de la Cruz, Miguel Cabrera (1648-1695), Public Domain

Week 10: Bain News Service, publisher - This image is available from the United States Library of Congress's Prints and Photographs divisionunder the digital ID ggbain.05091, Public Domain,

Week 12: Plato. Luni marble, copy of the portrait made by Silanion ca. 370 BC for the Academia in Athens. From the sacred area in Largo Argentina.Capitoline Museum, Public Domain

Week 13: Jerry Pinkney signing one of his many Caldecott Honor winning books at the Mazza Museum at The University of Findlay. Alvintrusty. November 2011 Fair Use https://creativecommons.org/licenses/by-sa/3.0/

Week 14: Mum Bett, aka Elizabeth Freeman, aged 70. Painted by Susan Ridley Sedgwick, aged 23. Watercolor on ivory, painted circa 1812. Photo courtesy of Massachusetts Historical Society, Boston, Public Domain

Week 15: Katherine Johnson, also Katherine Coleman Goble Johnson, 1983, Public Domain

Week 16: Maria Tallchief and Erik Bruhn from the front cover of Dance Magazine, July 1961, Public Domain

HISTORICAL FIGURE ARTWORK/PHOTO CREDIT

Week 17: Thomas Andrew Dorsey (July 1, 1899 – January 23, 1993), US gospel musician and blues pianist. Source: http://www.findagrave.com/cgi-bin/fg.cgi?page=gr&GRid=6546 Fair Use

Week 18: Sophie Brahe, unknown artist, 17 January 1602, Public Domain

 Week 19: Olaudah Equiano, aka Gustavus Vassa, unknown artist, First published in 1789, Public Domain

Week 20: Photo of Sophie Scholl Munich 1942, Public Domain